Rockschool Guita

Companion Guide

Acknowledgements

Published by Rockschool Ltd. © 2007

Catalogue Number: RSK100601

Compiled by: Simon Troup

Edited by: Simon Pitt & Peter Scott

Music engraving and layouts: Simon & Jennie Troup www.DigitalMusicArt.com

Audio production: Joe Bennett & Simon Troup

Syllabus Manager: Jeremy Ward

Cover design: Gillian Harding www.fuelcreativity.com

Printed and bound in the United Kingdom by Caligraving Ltd, Thetford, Norfolk

CDs manufactured in the United Kingdom by Branded Media Ltd, Basingstoke, Hampshire

Exclusive Distributors: Music Sales Ltd www.musicroom.com

Visit the Rockschool website at www.rockschool.co.uk

Telephone: 020 8332 6303

Fax: 020 8332 6297

Welcome to the Rockschool Guitar Companion Guide

Welcome to the Rockschool *Companion Guide* for Guitar. This *Companion Guide* is designed to give teachers, learners and candidates multiple examples of the unseen tests that are to be found within each Rockschool grade exam from Grades 1 to 8. The *Companion Guide* contains three to six examples of each of the following tests:

- Sight Reading (Grades 1-5)

- Improvisation & Interpretation (Grades 1-5)*

- Ear Tests (Grades 1-8)*

- Quick Study Pieces (Grades 6-8)*

All of the test examples marked (*) can be found on the audio CDs accompanying this *Companion Guide*. The quick study pieces (QSPs) come in two audio versions: one with a full mix of the QSP, and one with the guitar part removed. Please refer to the track listings given in the text.

In addition, you will find examples of the kinds of general musicianship questions that candidates are asked in each grade exam from Grades 1-8.

Teachers, learners and candidates should also refer to the Rockschool *Syllabus Guide* for Guitar where they will find the technical specifications for each section of the exam syllabus, including those parts (the performance pieces and the technical exercises) not covered by this *Companion Guide*. The Guitar specifications can be found in the *Guitar, Bass and Drums Syllabus Guide* on pages 6-15. References to the relevant sections of the Guitar *Syllabus Guide* can be found in each section below.

The purpose of the *Companion Guide* is to give candidates practice examples of the kinds of tests they will encounter in the exam. In the case of the sight reading, improvisation & interpretation and ear tests, we have created examples within each grade that offer candidates a progressive level of difficulty within a single grade: the first test example will be relatively simple when compared with the actual tests used in the exam, while the last example will be relatively more difficult. We have done this with the aim of aiding candidate confidence when faced with the tests in the exam.

If you have any queries about the syllabus for Guitar (or any other exam syllabus offered by Rockschool in bass guitar, drums, vocals, piano or our Music Practitioners qualifications) then please do not hesitate to call us on **020 8332 6303** or email us at: **info@rockschool.co.uk**. The Rockschool website, **www.rockschool.co.uk**, has detailed information on all aspects of our examinations, including examination regulations, detailed marking schemes and marking criteria as well as handy tips on how to get the most out of the performance pieces.

Sight Reading

Candidates attempting Grades 1-5 inclusive have a choice of taking either the sight reading or the improvisation & interpretation test in the exam. Six examples of the types of tests required in the exam are shown below. The full technical specifications of each test offered to candidates in the exam can be found in the Guitar *Syllabus Guide* on page 11. Please note that in Grades 4 and 5 each sight reading test also contains two bars of improvisation & interpretation.

You will be asked to prepare a sight reading test which is given to you by the examiner. This test may be in one of the following styles: blues or rock (Grades 1-3) or blues, rock, funk or jazz (Grades 4 & 5). The examiner will allow you 90 seconds to prepare the test and will set the tempo on a metronome. You can choose to play with or without the metronome. TAB fingerings are given along with standard notation in all sight reading tests.

Grade 1

The following examples are indicative of the types of test you will be given in the Grade 1 exam.

Example 1

Example 2

Example 3

Example 4

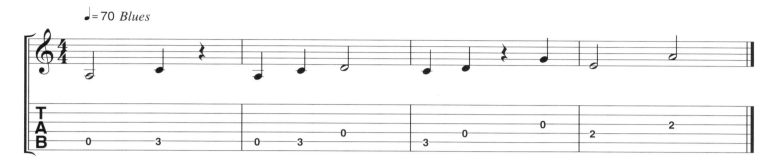

Example 5

Example 6

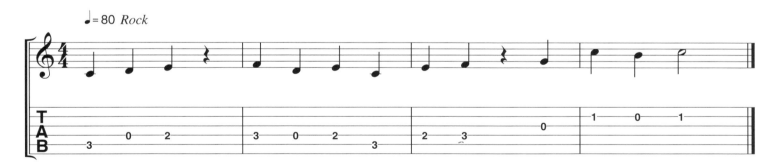

Grade 2

The following examples are indicative of the types of test you will be given in the Grade 2 exam.

Example 1

Example 2

Example 3

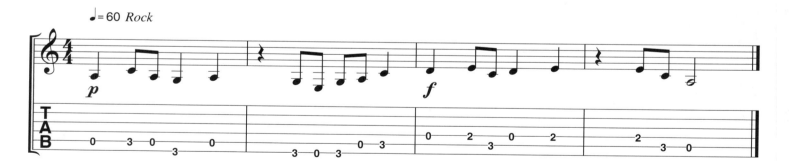

Example 4

Example 5

Example 6

Grade 3

The following examples are indicative of the types of test you will be given in the Grade 3 exam.

Example 1

Example 2

Example 3

Example 4

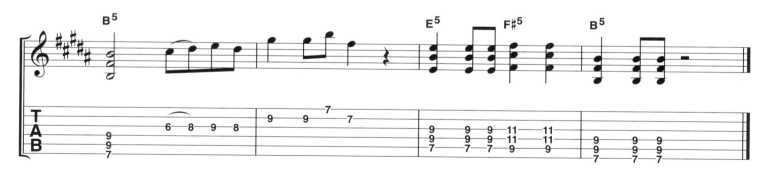

Example 5

Example 6

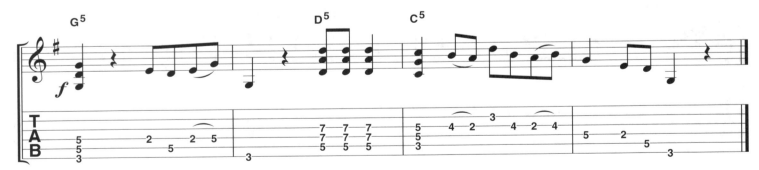

Grade 4

The following examples are indicative of the types of test you will be given in the Grade 4 exam. Please note that in Grade 4, the sight reading tests contain a small amount of improvisation & interpretation. This consists of a two bar section at the end of each test.

Example 1

Example 2

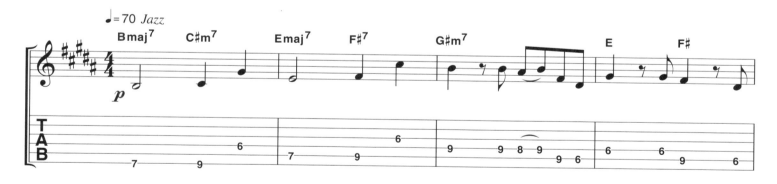

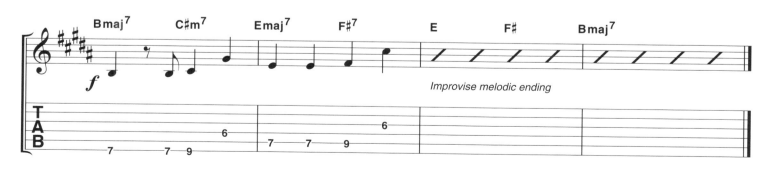

Example 3

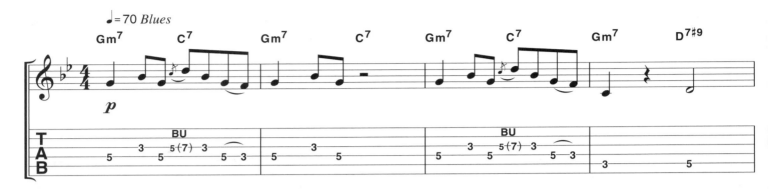

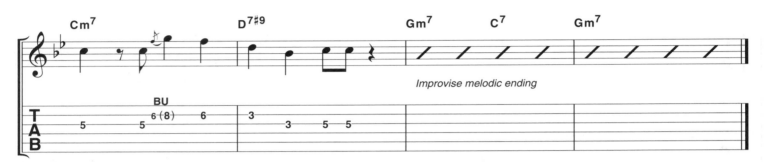

Example 4

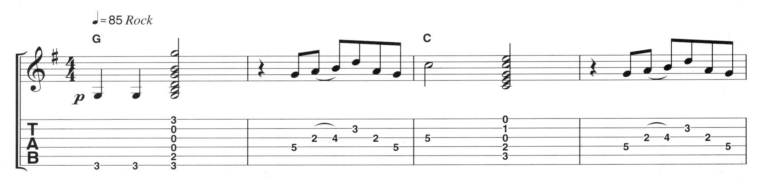

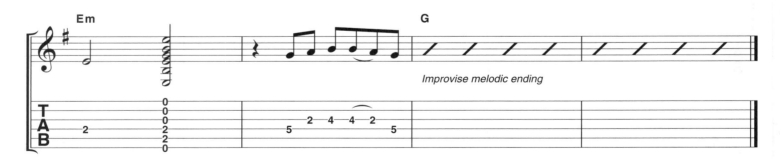

Example 5

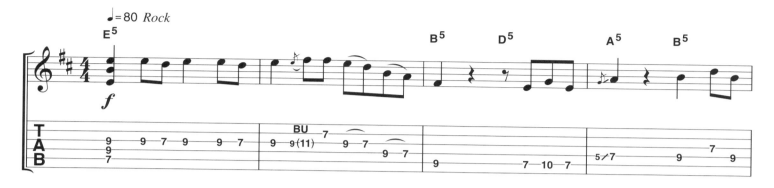

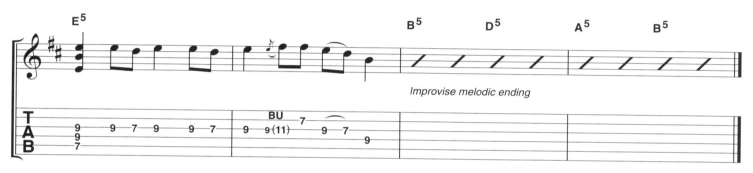

Example 6

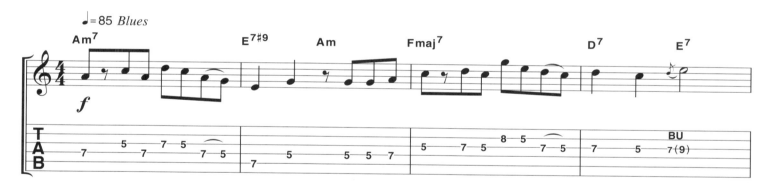

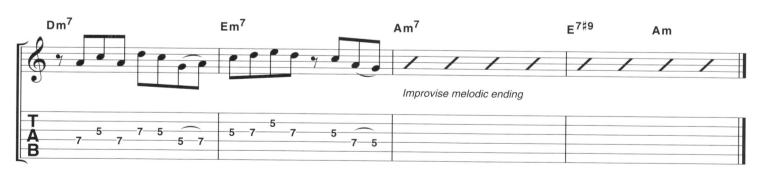

Grade 5

The following examples are indicative of the types of test you will be given in the Grade 5 exam. Please note that in Grade 5, the sight reading tests contain a small amount of improvisation & interpretation. This consists of a two bar section at the end of each test.

Example 1

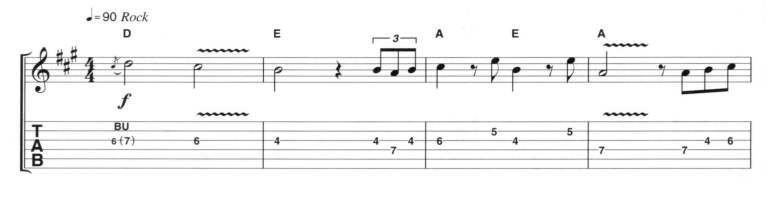

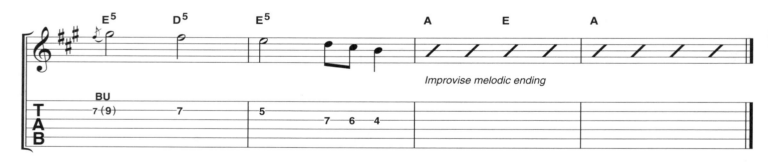

Example 2

Example 3

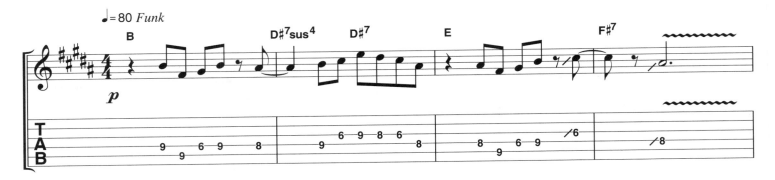

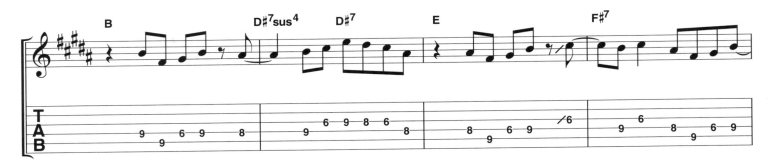

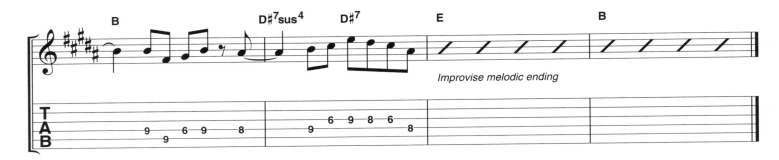

Example 4

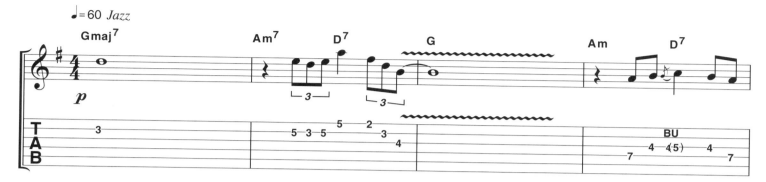

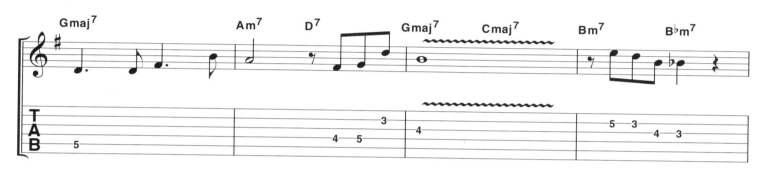

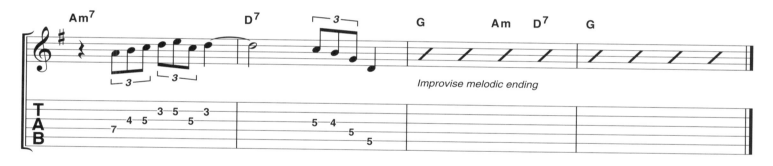

Improvise melodic ending

Example 5

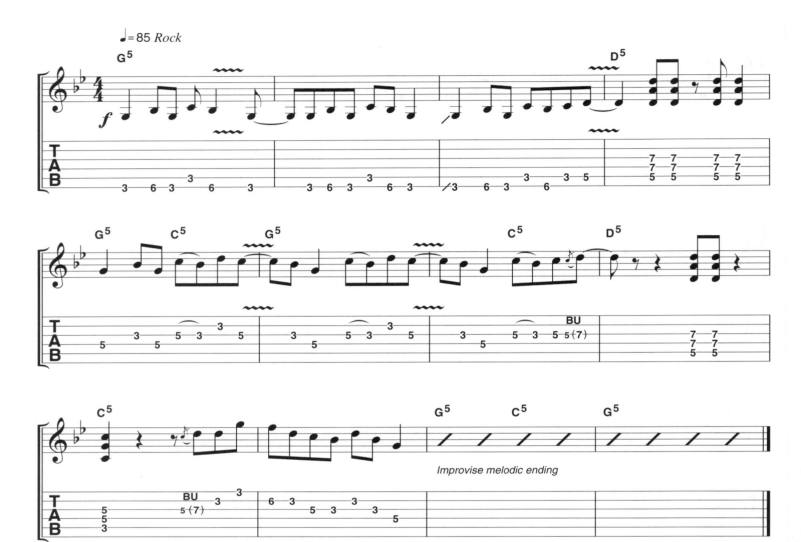

Improvise melodic ending

Example 6

Improvise melodic ending

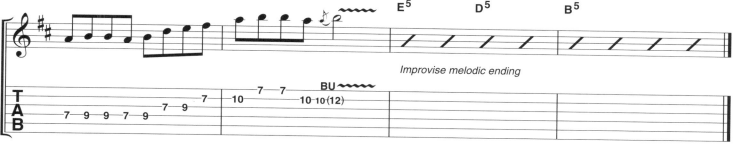

Improvisation & Interpretation

Candidates attempting Grades 1-5 inclusive have a choice of taking either the sight reading or the improvisation & interpretation test in the exam. Six examples of the types of tests required in the exam are shown below. The full technical specifications of each test offered to candidates in the exam can be found in the Guitar *Syllabus Guide* on page 12. Please note that in Grades 4 and 5 each improvisation & interpretation test also contains two bars of sight reading.

You will be asked to prepare an improvisation & interpretation test which is given to you by the examiner. This test may be in one of the following styles: blues or rock (Grades 1-3) or blues, rock, funk or jazz (Grades 4 & 5).

Grade 1

You will be asked to play an improvised line to a backing track of four bars. You may choose to play either rhythmic chords (first track per example) or a melodic lead line (second track per example). You have 30 seconds to prepare and then you will be allowed to practise through on the first playing of the backing track, before playing it to the examiner on the second playing of the backing track. This test is continuous with a one bar count in at the beginning and after the practice session.

Example 1   **CD 1 Tracks 1 & 2**

Example 2   **CD 1 Tracks 3 & 4**

Example 3   **CD 1 Tracks 5 & 6**

Example 4

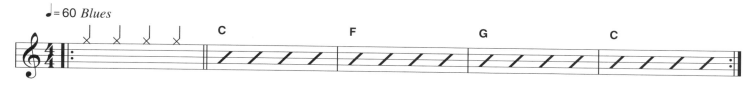

Example 5

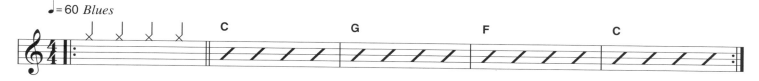

Example 6

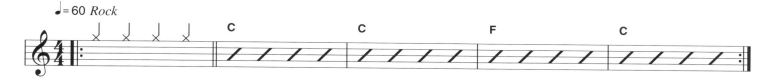

Grade 2

You will be asked to play an improvised line to a backing track of four bars. You may choose to play either rhythmic chords (first track per example) or a melodic lead line (second track per example). You have 30 seconds to prepare and then you will be allowed to practise through on the first playing of the backing track, before playing it to the examiner on the second playing of the backing track. This test is continuous with a one bar count in at the beginning and after the practice session.

Example 1   CD 1 Tracks 13 & 14

Example 2   CD 1 Tracks 15 & 16

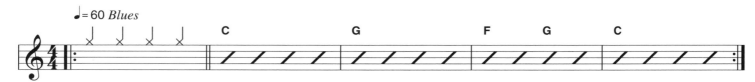

Example 3   CD 1 Tracks 17 & 18

Example 4

CD 1 Tracks 19 & 20

Example 5

CD 1 Tracks 21 & 22

Example 6

CD 1 Tracks 23 & 24

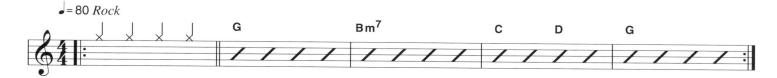

Grade 3

You will be asked to play an improvised line to a backing track of eight bars. You may choose to play either rhythmic chords (first track per example) or a melodic lead line (second track per example). You have 30 seconds to prepare and then you will be allowed to practise through on the first playing of the backing track, before playing it to the examiner on the second playing of the backing track. This test is continuous with a one bar count in at the beginning and after the practice session.

Example 1   **CD 1 Tracks 25 & 26**

Example 2   **CD 1 Tracks 27 & 28**

Example 3   **CD 1 Tracks 29 & 30**

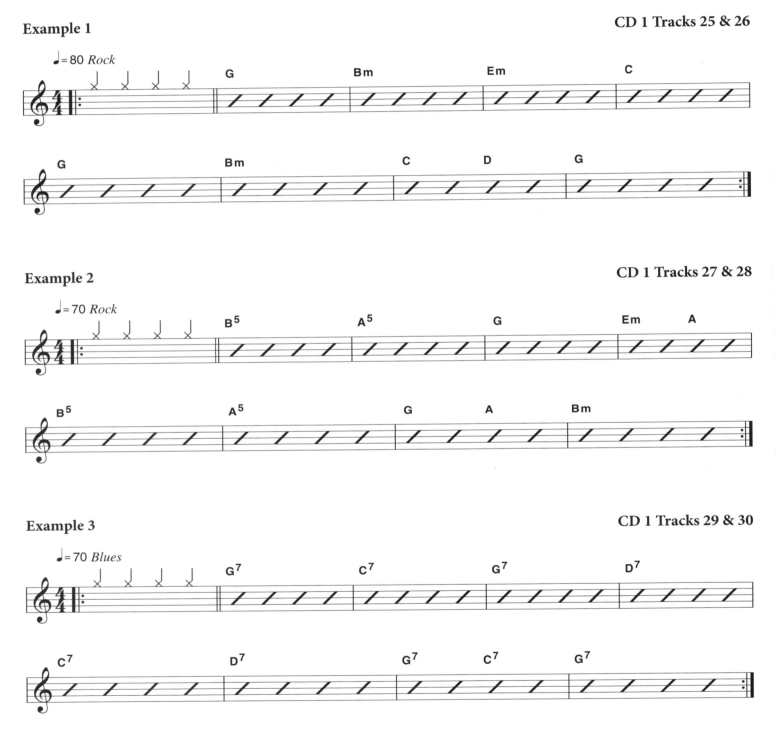

Example 4

CD 1 Tracks 31 & 32

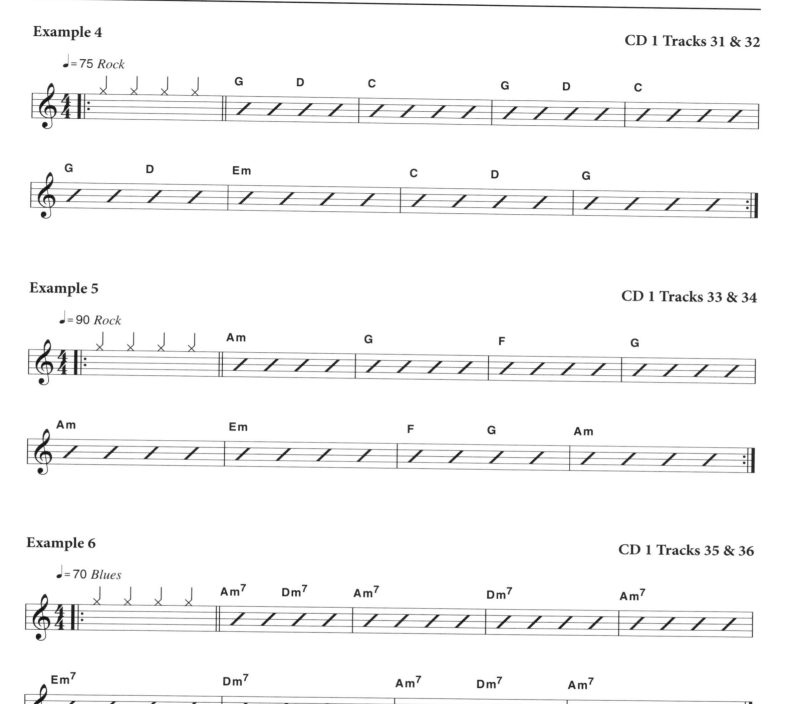

Example 5

CD 1 Tracks 33 & 34

Example 6

CD 1 Tracks 35 & 36

Grade 4

In Grade 4, the improvisation & interpretation tests contain a small amount of sight reading. This consists of a two bar section of rhythm notation to be found at the beginning of each test. You will be asked to play the chords in the rhythms indicated and complete the test using an improvised line made up of chords and lead lines where indicated. This is played to a backing track of no more than eight bars. You have 30 seconds to prepare and then you will be allowed to practise through on the first playing of the backing track, before playing it to the examiner on the second playing of the backing track. This test is continuous with a one bar count in at the beginning and after the practice session.

Example 1   CD 1 Track 37

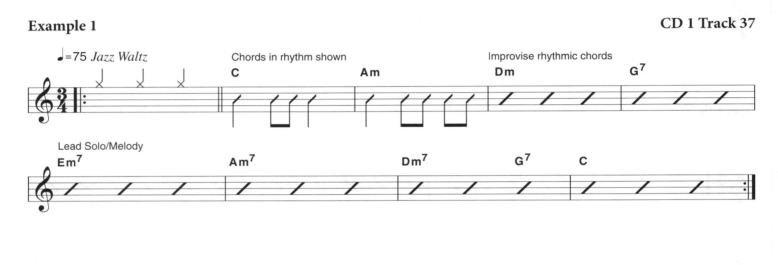

Example 2   CD 1 Track 38

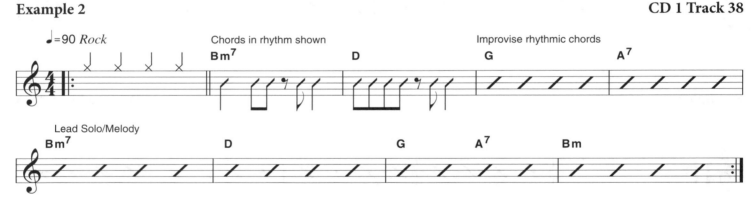

Example 3   CD 1 Track 39

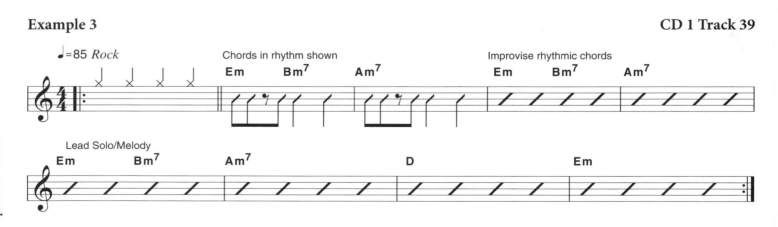

Example 4

CD 1 Track 40

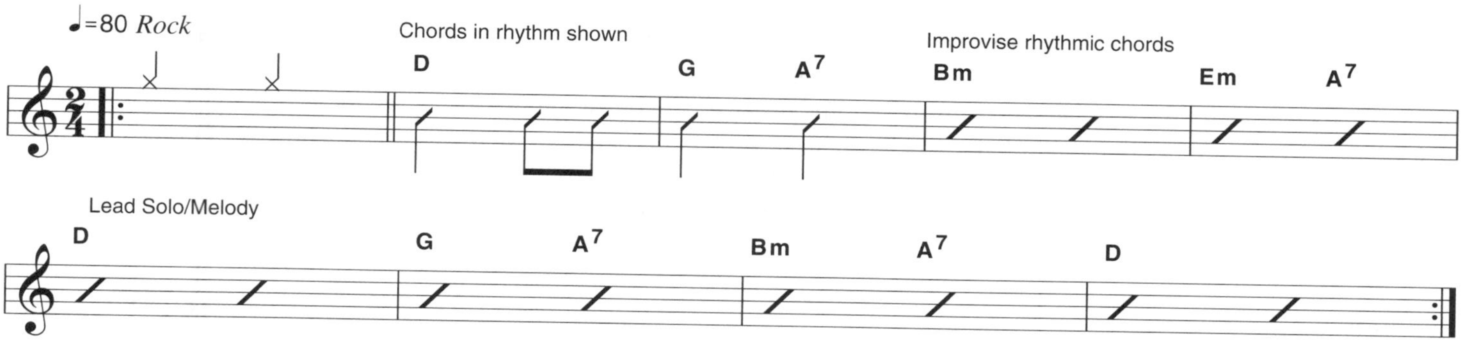

Example 5

CD 1 Track 41

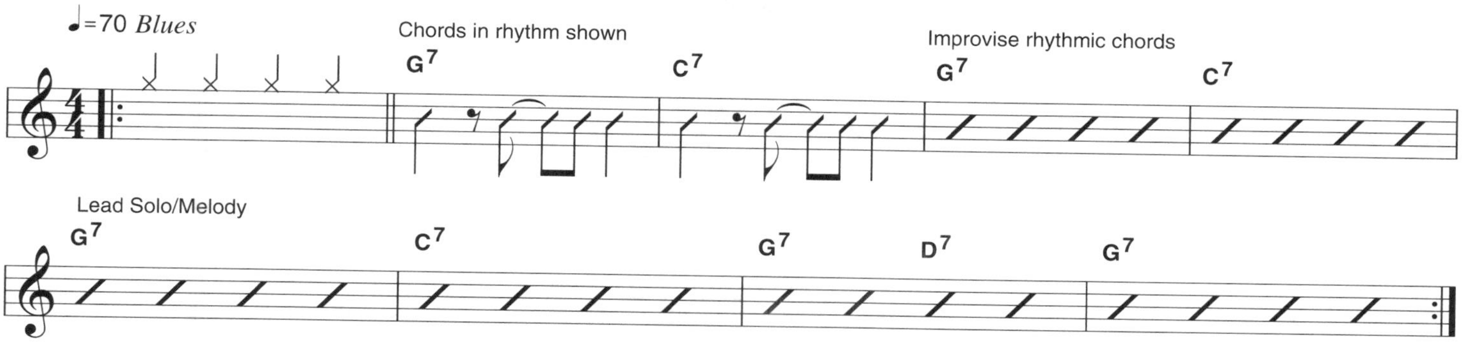

Example 6

CD 1 Track 42

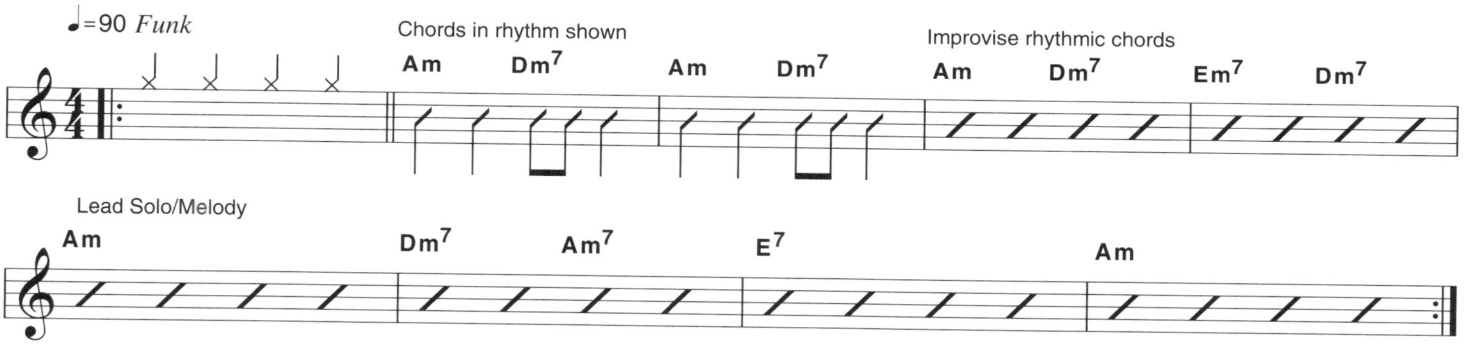

Grade 5

In Grade 5, the improvisation & interpretation tests contain a small amount of sight reading. This consists of a two bar section of rhythm notation to be found at the beginning of each test. You will be asked to play the chords in the rhythms indicated and complete the test using an improvised line made up of chords and lead lines where indicated. This is played to a backing track of no more than eight bars. You have 30 seconds to prepare and then you will be allowed to practise through on the first playing of the backing track, before playing it to the examiner on the second playing of the backing track. This test is continuous with a one bar count in at the beginning and after the practice session.

Example 1   **CD 1 Track 43**

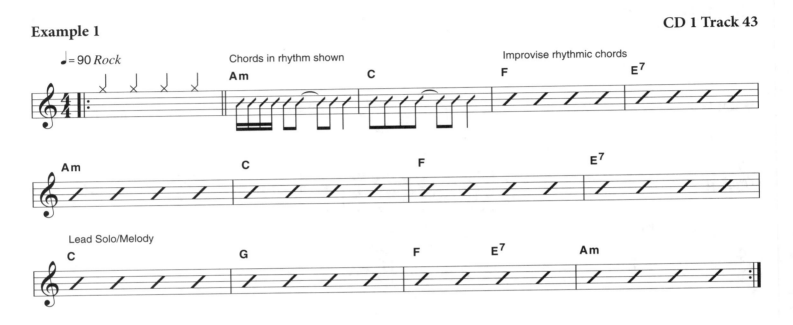

Example 2   **CD 1 Track 44**

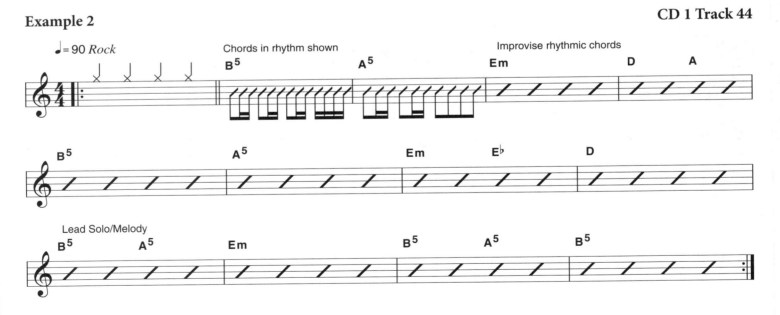

Example 3

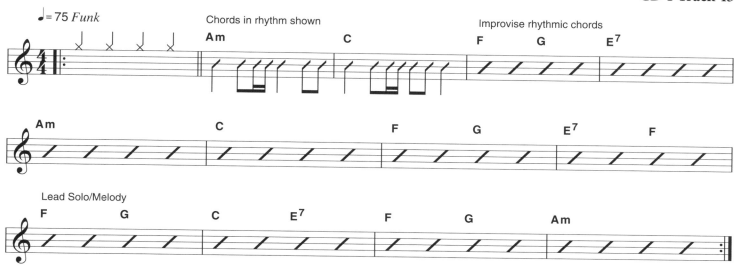

Example 4

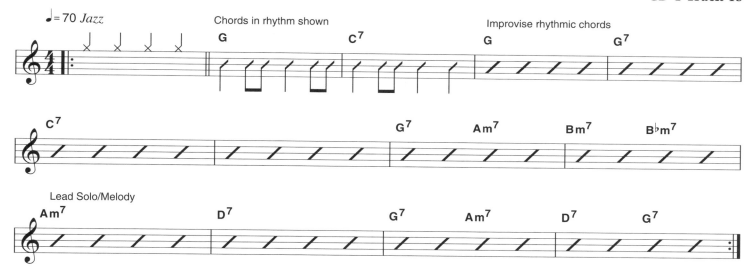

Example 5

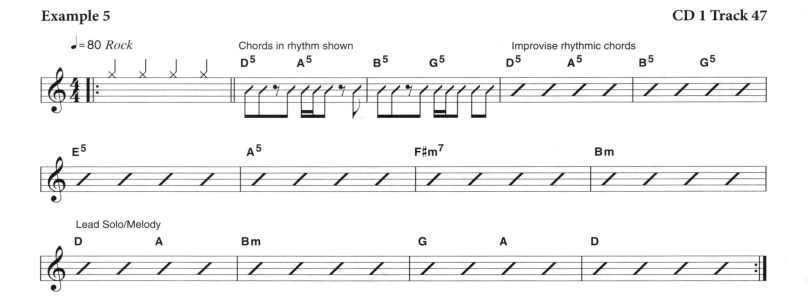

Example 6

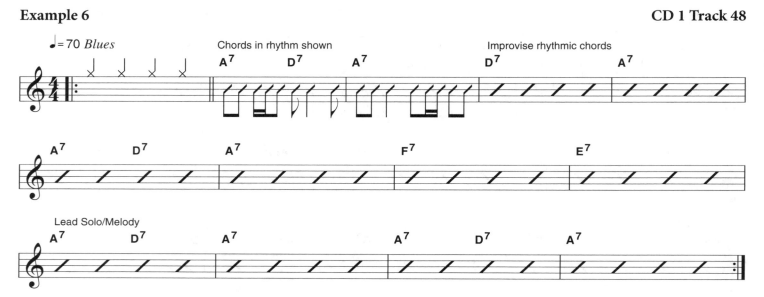

Ear Tests

You will be asked to play two ear tests in the exam. The tests are played on CD and use real instrument sounds. Each test is played to you by the examiner twice and you will play back each test to either a drum backing (grades 1-5) or a bass and drum backing (Grades 6-8). You may use your instrument while the CD is playing. Technical specifications for the ear tests can be found in the Guitar *Syllabus Guide* on pages 13-15.

Grade 1 Test 1: Melodic Recall

You will be asked to play back on your instrument a two bar melody composed from the first three notes of the C major scale (C, D & E). You will be given the tonic, told the starting note, and hear the test twice with drum backing. There is a short break in the test for you to practise and then the test will recommence. You will then play the melody in time to the drum backing. The test is continuous.

Example 1   CD 1 Track 49

Example 2   CD 1 Track 50

Example 3   CD 1 Track 51

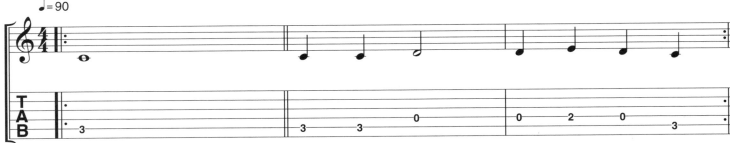

Example 4

CD 1 Track 52

Example 5

CD 1 Track 53

Example 6

CD 1 Track 54

Grade 1 Test 2: Rhythmic Recall

You will be asked to play back on your instrument a two bar rhythm played on the bottom E string on the guitar. The rhythm is played twice to a drum backing. There is a short break in the test to allow you to practise and the test will recommence. You will then play the rhythm in time to the drum backing. The test is continuous.

Example 1   **CD 1 Track 55**

Example 2   **CD 1 Track 56**

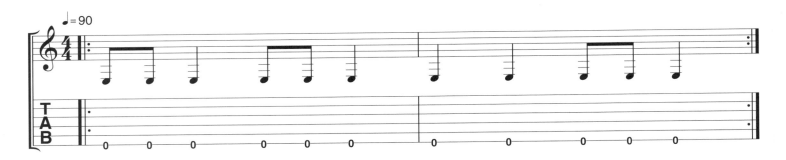

Example 3   **CD 1 Track 57**

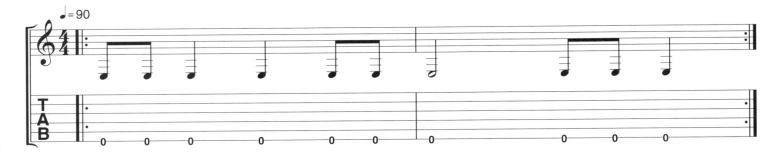

Example 4

CD 1 Track 58

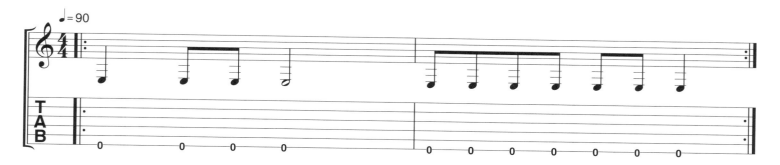

Example 5

CD 1 Track 59

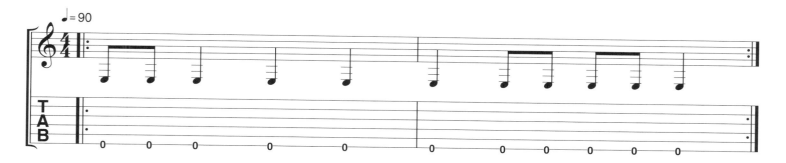

Example 6

CD 1 Track 60

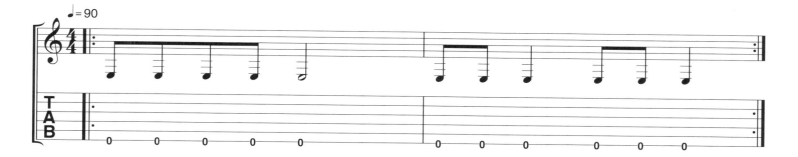

Grade 2 Test 1: Melodic Recall

You will be asked to play back on your instrument a two bar melody composed from either the C or G minor pentatonic scales. You will be given the tonic, told the key, and hear the test twice with drum backing. There is a short break in the test to allow you to practise and then the test will recommence. You will then play the melody in time to the drum backing. The test is continuous.

Example 1

CD 1 Track 61

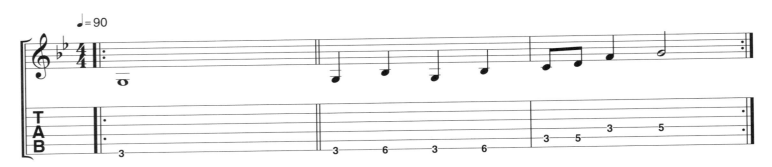

Example 2

CD 1 Track 62

Example 3

CD 1 Track 63

Example 4

CD 1 Track 64

Example 5

CD 1 Track 65

Example 6

CD 1 Track 66

Grade 2 Test 2: Rhythmic Recall

You will be asked to play back on your instrument a two bar rhythm played on an open E minor7 chord. The rhythm is played twice to a drum backing. There is a short break in the test for the candidate to practise and the test will recommence. You will then play the rhythm in time to the drum backing. The test is continuous.

Example 1
CD 1 Track 67

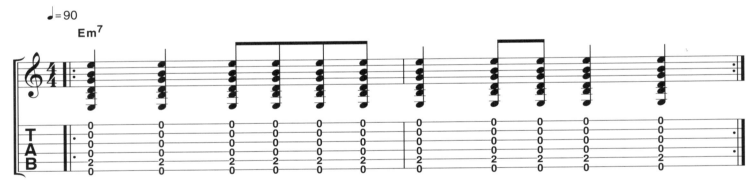

Example 2
CD 1 Track 68

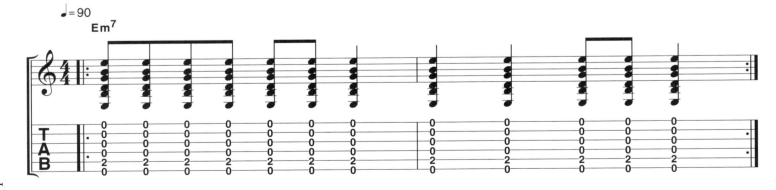

Example 3
CD 1 Track 69

Example 4

CD 1 Track 70

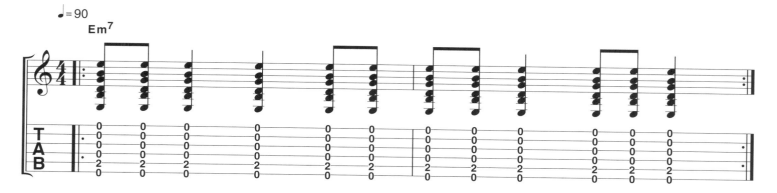

Example 5

CD 1 Track 71

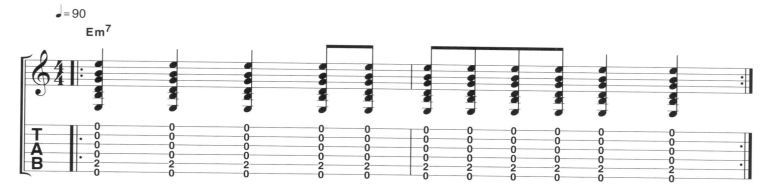

Example 6

CD 1 Track 72

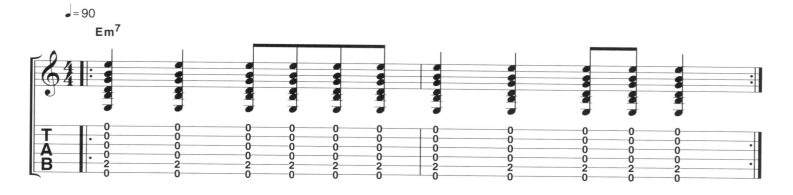

Grade 3 Test 1: Melodic Recall

You will be asked to play back on your instrument a four bar melody composed from the G major scale or the G minor pentatonic scale. You will be given the tonic, told the key, and hear the test twice with drum backing. There is a short break in the test for you to practise and the test will recommence. You will then play the melody in time to the drum backing. The test is continuous.

Example 1

CD 2 Track 1

Example 2

CD 2 Track 2

Example 3

CD 2 Track 3

Example 4

Example 5

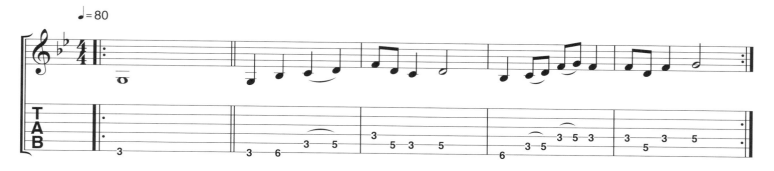

Example 6

Grade 3 Test 2: Chord & Rhythm Recall

You will be asked to play back on your instrument a four bar rhythmic chord sequence played on the guitar. You will be told the tonic chord and the piece will be played twice with a drum backing. There is a short break in the test to allow you to practise and the test will recommence. You will then play back the rhythmic chord sequence in time to the drum backing. The test is continuous. The test will use chord types and keys found in the technical work up to and including the appropriate grade.

Example 1

CD 2 Track 7

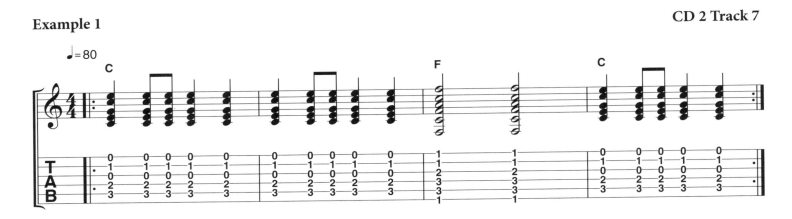

Example 2

CD 2 Track 8

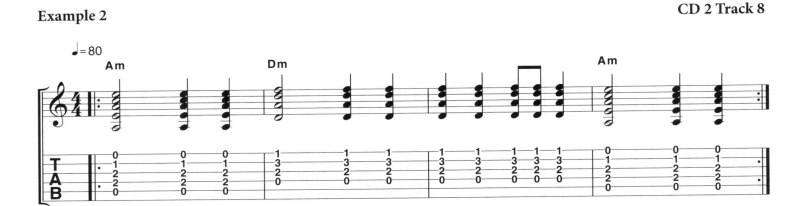

Example 3

CD 2 Track 9

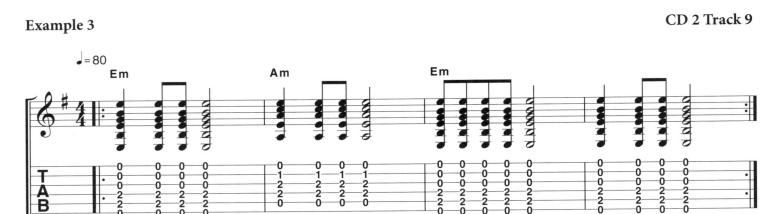

Example 4

CD 2 Track 10

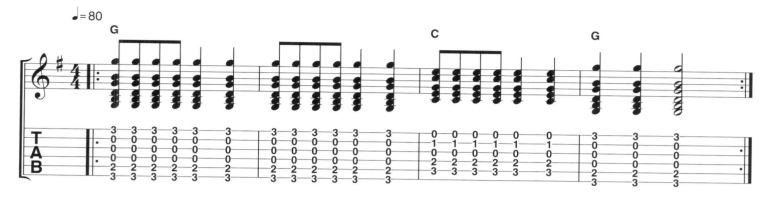

Example 5

CD 2 Track 11

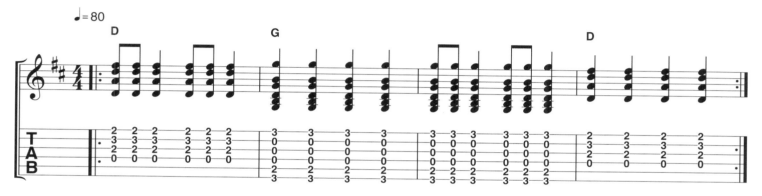

Example 6

CD 2 Track 12

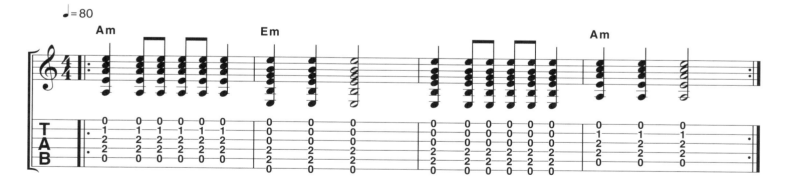

Grade 4 Test 1: Melodic Recall

You will be asked to play back on your instrument a four bar melody composed from the C major or C minor scales. You will be given the tonic note, told the key and the starting note. The test is played twice to a drum backing. There is a short break in the test for you to practise and the test will recommence. You will then play the melody in time to the drum backing. The test is continuous.

Example 1

CD 2 Track 13

Example 2

CD 2 Track 14

Example 3

CD 2 Track 15

Example 4

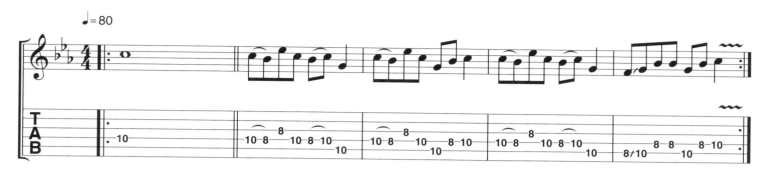

Example 5

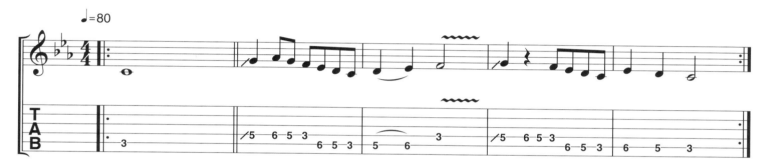

Example 6

Grade 4 Test 2: Chord & Rhythm Recall

You will be asked to play back on your instrument a four bar rhythmic chord sequence played on the guitar. You will be told the tonic chord and the piece will be played twice with a drum backing. There is a short break in the test to allow you to practise and the test will recommence. You will then play back the rhythmic chord sequence in time to the drum backing. The test is continuous. The test will use chord types and keys found in the technical work up to and including the appropriate grade.

Example 1   CD 2 Track 19

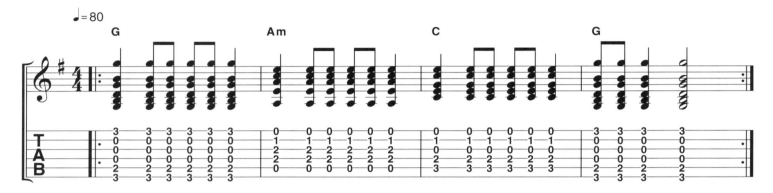

Example 2   CD 2 Track 20

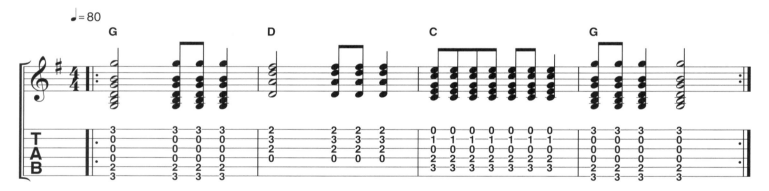

Example 3   CD 2 Track 21

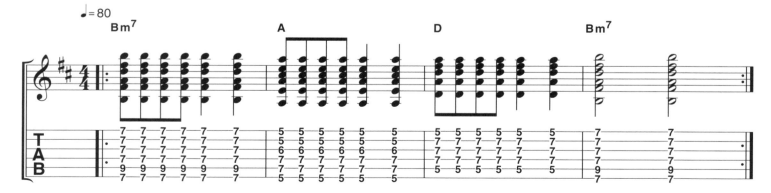

Example 4

CD 2 Track 22

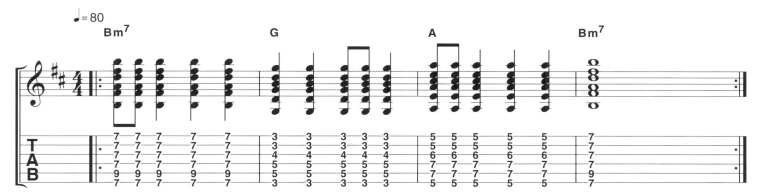

Example 5

CD 2 Track 23

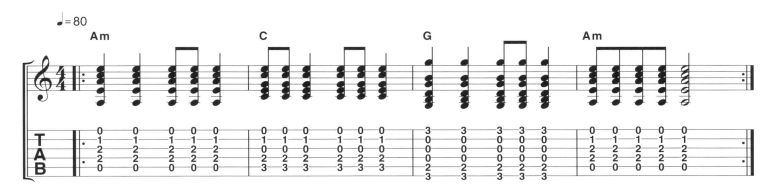

Example 6

CD 2 Track 24

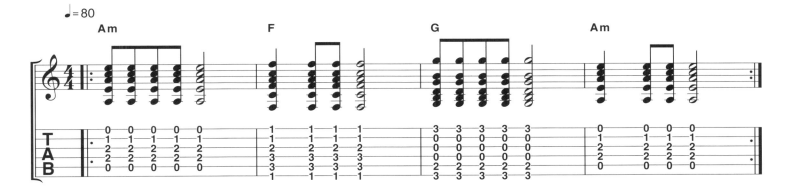

Grade 5 Test 1: Melodic Recall

You will be asked to play back on your instrument a four bar melody composed from the G, A or B minor pentatonic scales. You will be given the tonic note and be told the key and the starting note. The test is played twice to a drum backing. There is a short break in the test for you to practise and the test will recommence. You will then play the melody in time to the drum backing. The test is continuous.

Example 1

CD 2 Track 25

Example 2

CD 2 Track 26

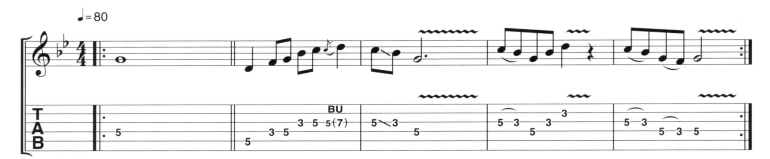

Example 3

CD 2 Track 27

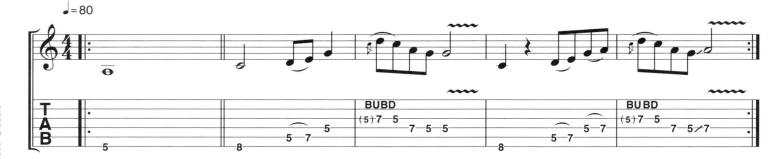

Example 4

Example 5

Example 6

Grade 5 Test 2: Chord & Rhythm Recall

You will be asked to play back on your instrument a four bar rhythmic chord sequence played on the guitar. You will be told the tonic chord and the piece will be played twice with a drum backing. There is a short break in the test to allow you to practise and the test will recommence. You will then play back the rhythmic chord sequence in time to the drum backing. The test is continuous. The test will use chord types and keys found in the technical work up to and including the appropriate grade.

Example 1 CD 2 Track 31

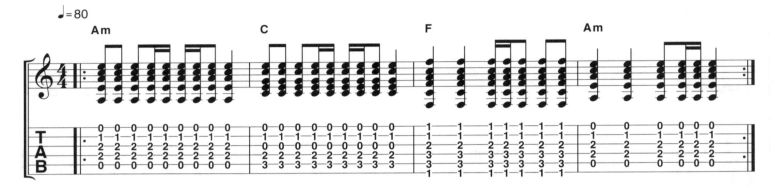

Example 2 CD 2 Track 32

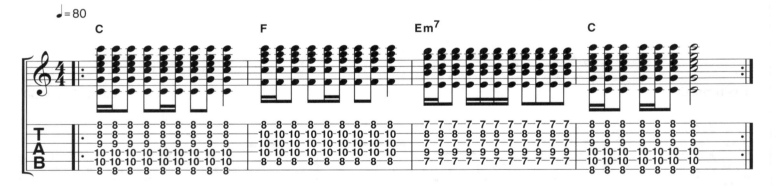

Example 3 CD 2 Track 33

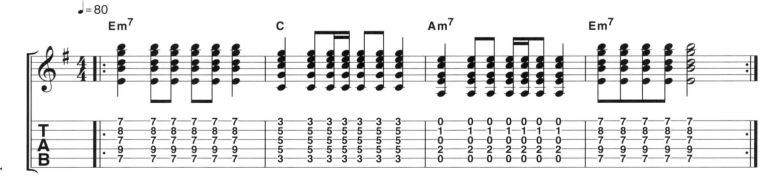

Example 4

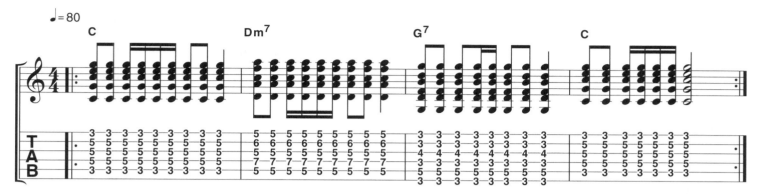

Example 5

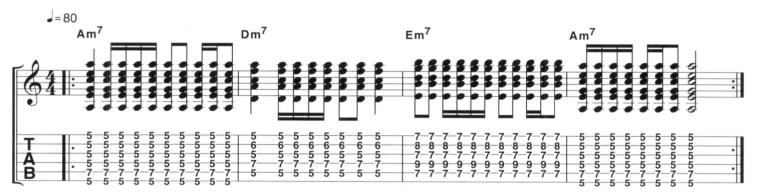

Example 6

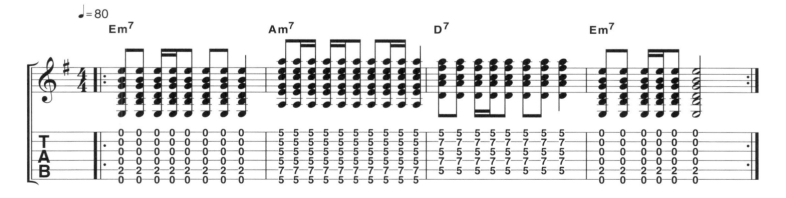

Grade 6 Test 1: Melodic Recall

You will be asked to play back on your instrument a four bar melody composed from the G, A or B Ionian mode. You will be given the tonic note and the key. The test is played twice to a bass and drum backing. There is a short break in the test for you to practise and the test will recommence. You will then play the melody in time to the bass and drum backing. The test is continuous.

Example 1   CD 2 Track 37

Example 2   CD 2 Track 38

Example 3   CD 2 Track 39

Example 4

CD 2 Track 40

Example 5

CD 2 Track 41

Example 6

CD 2 Track 42

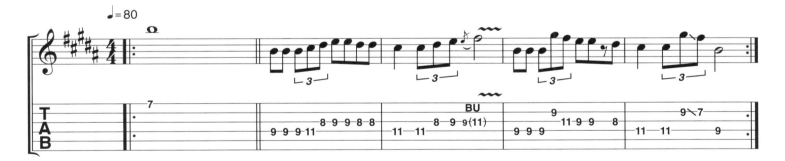

Grade 6 Test 2: Chord & Rhythm Recall

You will be asked to play back on your instrument a four bar rhythmic chord sequence played on the guitar. You will be told the tonic chord and the piece will be played twice with a drum backing. There is a short break in the test to allow you to practise and the test will recommence. You will then play back the rhythmic chord sequence in time to the drum backing. The test is continuous. The test will use chord types and keys found in the technical work up to and including the appropriate grade.

Example 1   CD 2 Track 43

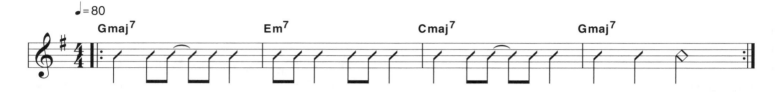

Example 2   CD 2 Track 44

Example 3   CD 2 Track 45

Example 4

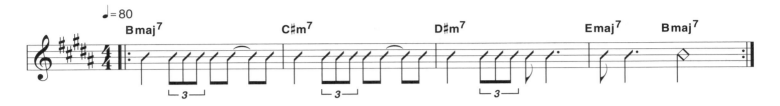

Example 5

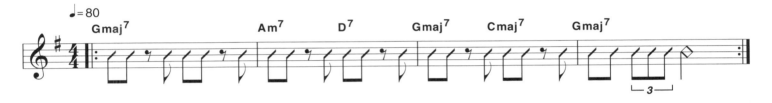

Example 6

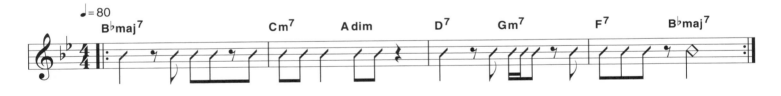

Grade 7 Test 1: Melodic Recall

You will be asked to play back on your instrument a four bar melody composed from the G, A or B Aeolian mode. You will be given the tonic note and the key. The test is played twice to a bass and drum backing. There is a short break in the test for you to practise and the test will recommence. You will then play the melody in time to the bass and drum backing. The test is continuous.

Example 1

CD 3 Track 1

Example 2

CD 3 Track 2

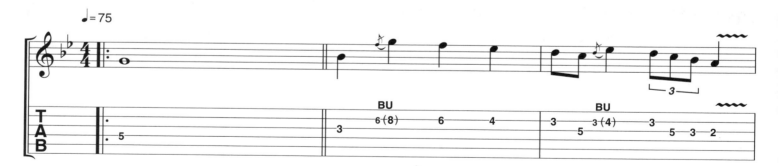

Example 3

CD 3 Track 3

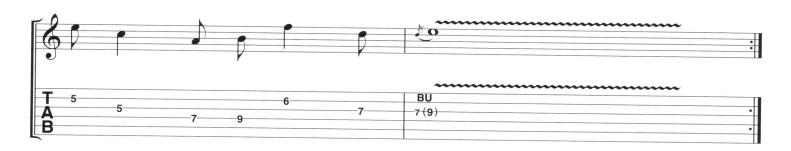

Example 4

CD 3 Track 4

Example 5

CD 3 Track 5

Example 6

CD 3 Track 6

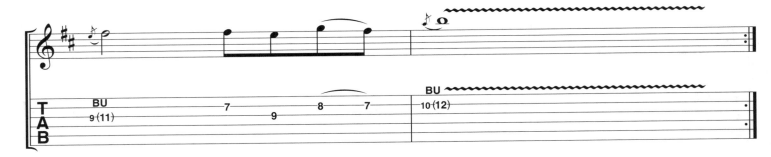

Grade 7 Test 2: Chord & Rhythm Recall

You will be asked to play back on your instrument a four bar rhythmic chord sequence played on the guitar. You will be told the tonic chord and the piece will be played twice with a drum backing. There is a short break in the test to allow you to practise and the test will recommence. You will then play back the rhythmic chord sequence in time to the drum backing. The test is continuous. The test will use chord types and keys found in the technical work up to and including the appropriate grade.

Example 1   CD 3 Track 7

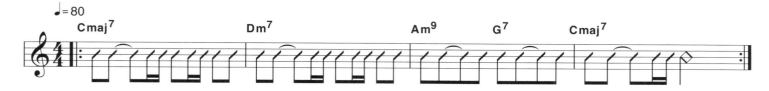

Example 2   CD 3 Track 8

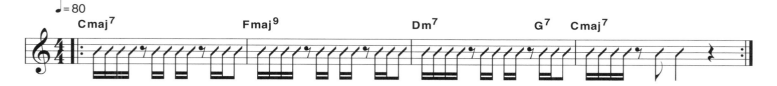

Example 3   CD 3 Track 9

Example 4

CD 3 Track 10

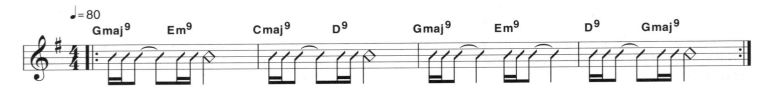

Example 5

CD 3 Track 11

Example 6

CD 3 Track 12

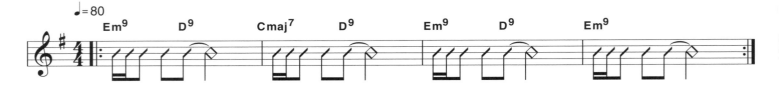

Grade 8 Test 1: Melodic Recall

You will be asked to play back on your instrument a four bar melody composed from the G, A or B Dorian or Mixolydian modes. You will be given the tonic note and the key. The test is played twice to a bass and drum backing. There is a short break in the test for you to practise and the test will recommence. You will then play the melody in time to the bass and drum backing. The test is continuous.

Example 1: B Dorian

CD 3 Track 13

Example 2: G Mixolydian

CD 3 Track 14

Example 3: A Dorian

CD 3 Track 15

Example 4: G Dorian

CD 3 Track 16

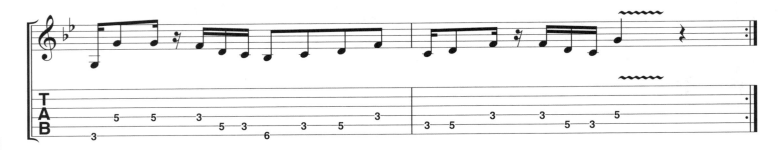

Example 5: B Mixolydian

CD 3 Track 17

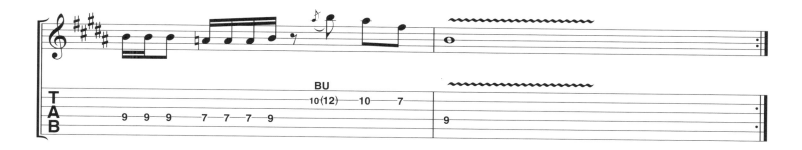

Example 6: A Mixolydian

CD 3 Track 18

Grade 8 Test 2: Chord & Rhythm Recall

You will be asked to play back on your instrument a four bar rhythmic chord sequence played on the guitar. You will be told the tonic chord and the piece will be played twice with a drum backing. There is a short break in the test to allow you to practise and the test will recommence. You will then play back the rhythmic chord sequence in time to the drum backing. The test is continuous. The test will use chord types and keys found in the technical work up to and including the appropriate grade.

Example 1   CD 3 Track 19

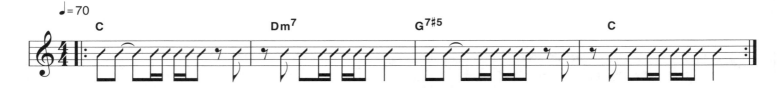

Example 2   CD 3 Track 20

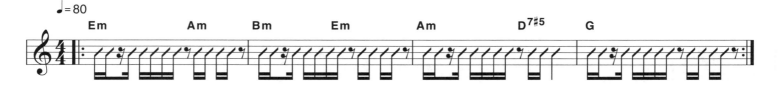

Example 3   CD 3 Track 21

Example 4

CD 3 Track 22

Example 5

CD 3 Track 23

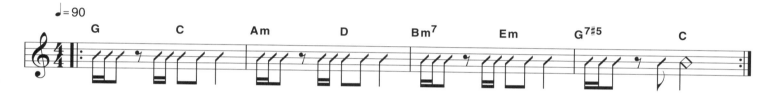

Example 6

CD 3 Track 24

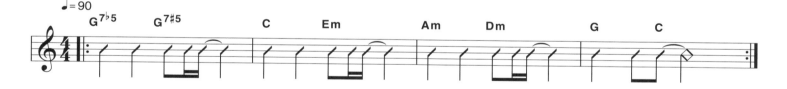

Quick Study Pieces

A quick study piece (QSP) is played in the Grade 6, 7 and 8 exams. You will be given a QSP to prepare 20 minutes before entering the examination room and you are asked to arrive at the exam centre at least half an hour before your examination time to give yourself enough time to practise.

You will be asked to perform the QSP from a paper outline and a CD given to you by the examiner. The outline is in the form of a 'lead sheet' or 'session chart' and will contain information on style, tempo and length, along with other musical information such as dynamics and marked solo passages. The QSP is written in standard notation, TAB fingerings and chord notation.

The CD contains a backing track to be used for both practice and performance in the examination. Each QSP will be in one of the following styles: rock, funk, blues or jazz. The performance should reflect the style of the piece and you should use the 'spaces' in the music to develop your musical ideas.

The full technical specifications for the QSPs can be found in the Guitar *Syllabus Guide* on pages 12-13. There are three practice examples of the QSPs by grade shown below and there are two audio tracks on the CD for each one. The first track contains an 'idealised' version of the QSP, while the second track is the backing track for you to play along to.

Grade 6 Example 1

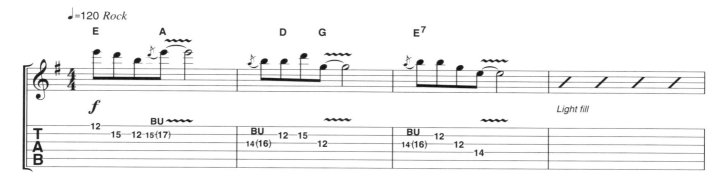

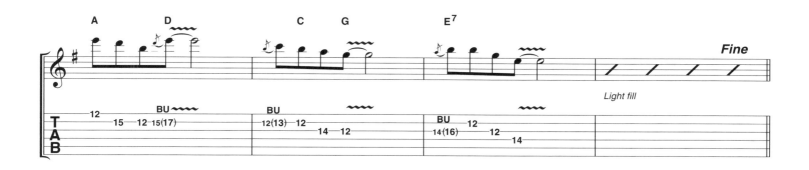

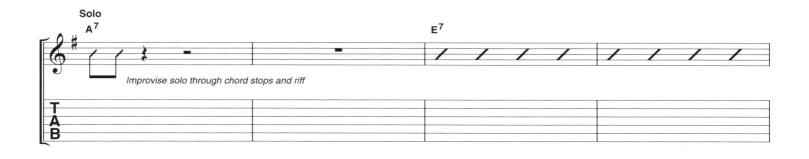

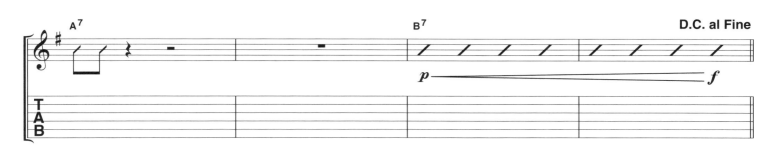

Grade 6 Example 2

CD 3 Tracks 27 & 28

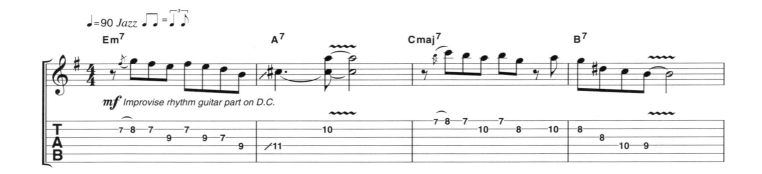

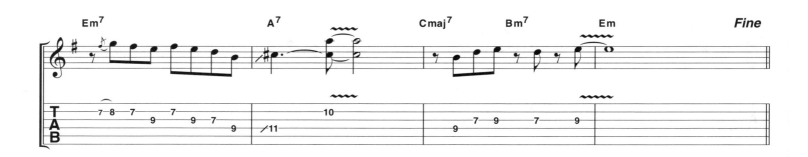

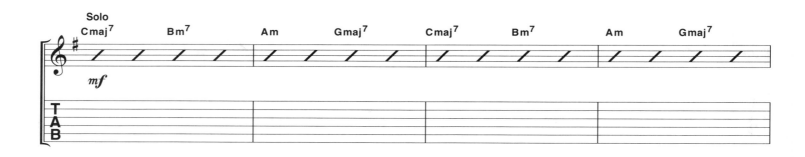

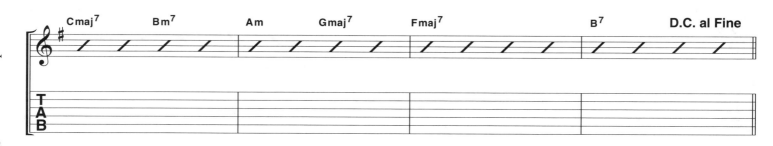

Grade 6 Example 3

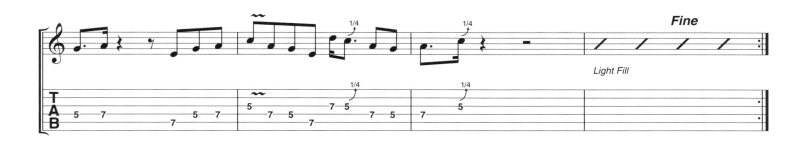

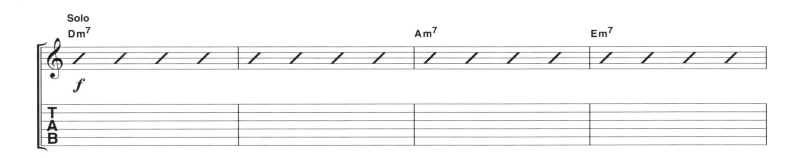

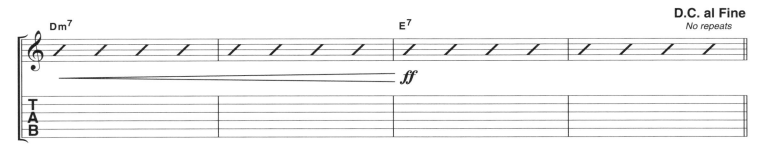

Grade 7 Example 1

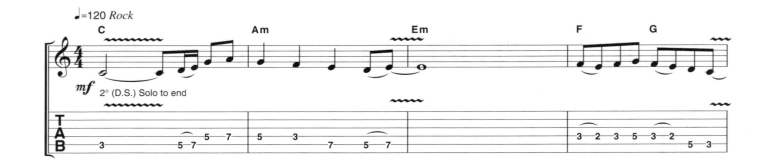

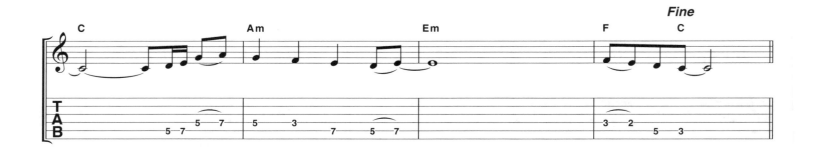

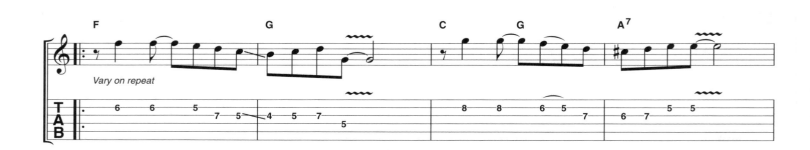

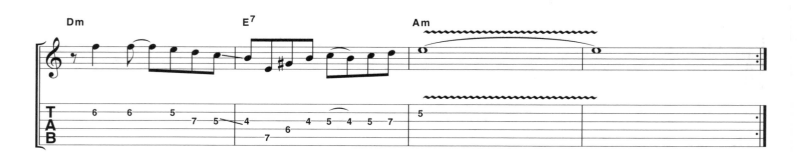

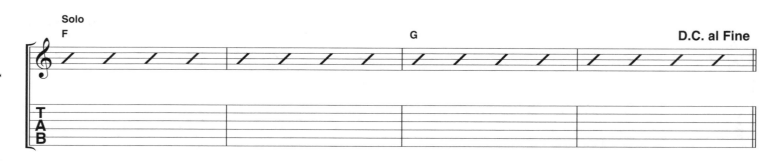

Grade 7 Example 2

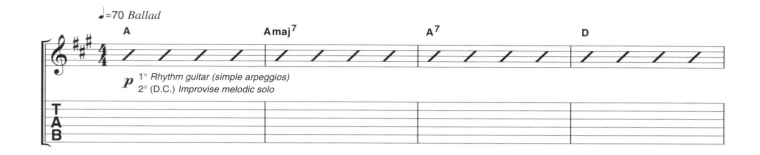

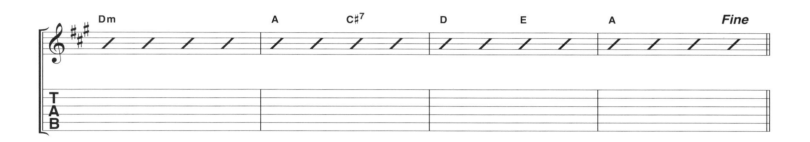

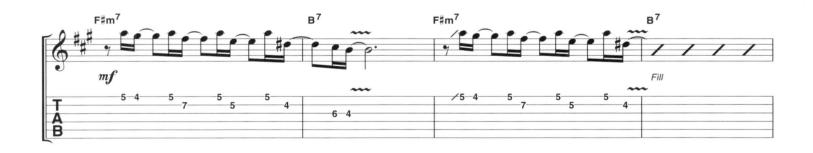

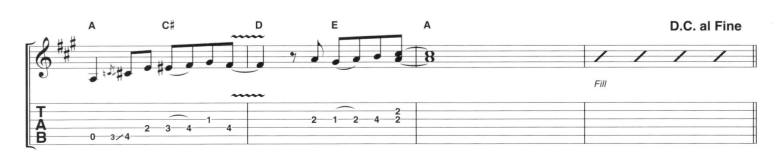

Grade 7 Example 3

1° *Play given melody*
2° *Develop melody*
3° *(D.C.) Improvise simple rhythm guitar part*

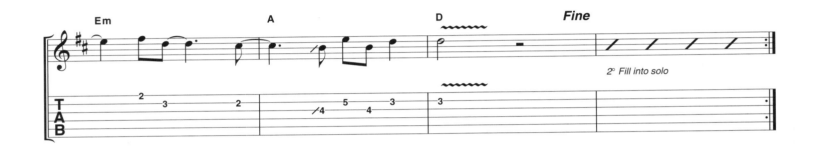

Fine

2° *Fill into solo*

Solo

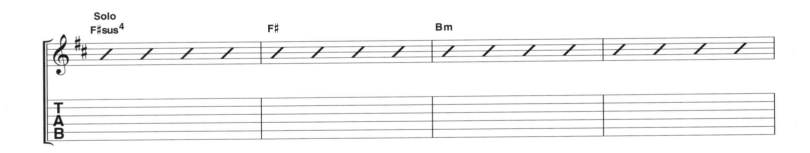

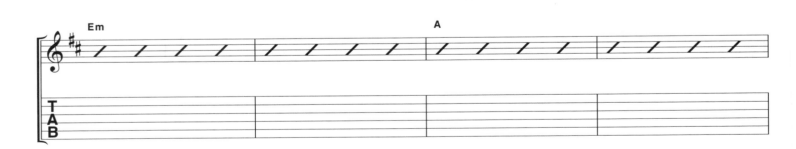

D.C. al Fine

Grade 8 Example 1

Grade 8 Example 2

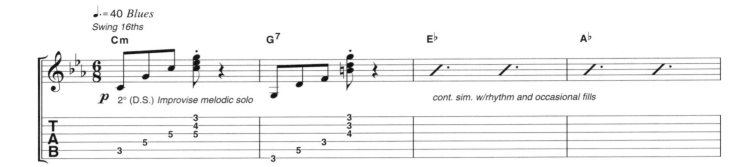

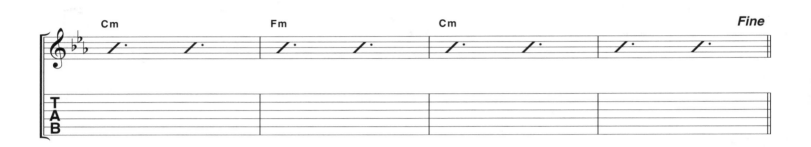

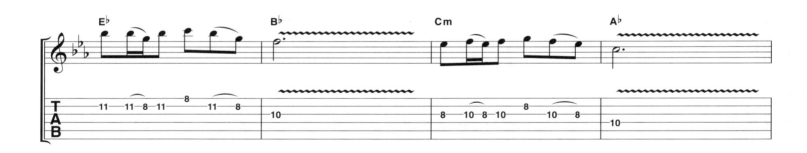

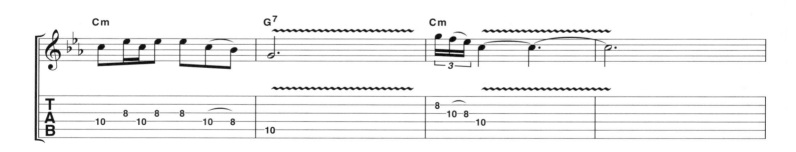

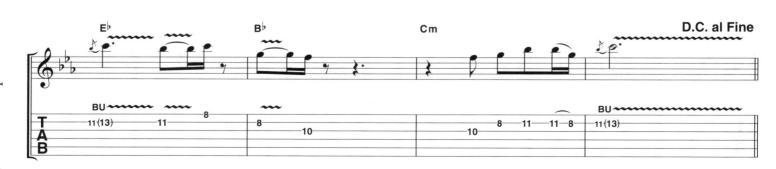

Grade 8 Example 3

General Musicianship Questions

Each Rockschool grade exam ends with five questions asked by the examiner. The examiner will ask you these questions using a piece played by you as a starting point. In Grades 1-6, you will be asked questions in two main areas: (i) music notation and (ii) knowledge of the guitar (including amplification). Grades 7 & 8 will include a third category of question concerning history and style.

Here are some sample questions that are typically asked by Rockschool's examiners grade by grade, along with sample answers typically given by candidates. As a general rule, in Grades 1-3, examiners will ask candidates 4 questions on the music notation and one instrument question. In Grades 4-6 the instrument knowledge questions may also include cover guitar amplification and effects. In Grades 7 & 8 you can expect questions to cover all three categories of notation, style and instrument knowledge. Please note that these are indicative questions and some may be asked in more than one grade.

Grade 1

The theory questions here refer to the performance piece 'Head On', page 5.

Q: What does 4/4 mean?
A: Four quarter (crotchet) notes in a bar

Q: How many beats is that note worth (examiner selects a half (minim) note)?
A: Two beats

Q: What is the pitch of the first note?
A: E

Q: What is the difference between a major and a minor chord?
A: A major chord sounds 'happy' and a minor chord sounds 'sad' OR A major chord has a major third and a minor chord has a minor third

Instrumental question:
Q: Where is/are: the nut/pick-ups/neck/frets on your guitar?

Grade 2

The theory questions here refer to the performance piece 'Blue Phones', page 8.

Q: What do we call the two notes played at the beginning?
A: Eighth (quaver) notes

Q: What does 'ƒ' mean?
A: Loud (*forte*)

Q: What value is the rest in the first bar of line two?
A: Eighth (quaver) note rest

Q: what do these signs mean in bar 10?
A: Repeat marks: play the same bar again

Q: How is a major chord made up?
A: A root note (1st note), major third (3rd note), perfect fifth (5th note) of the major scale

Instrument question:
Q: What do the volume and tone controls do?
A: The volume makes the sound louder or softer. The tone control gives more treble or more bass, depending on the setting.

Grade 3

The theory questions here refer to the performance piece 'Been There', pages 6-7.

Q: What do the symbols at the beginning of the first bar refer to?
A: The key signature

Q: What is the value of the final rest in the last bar?
A: Two beats (half note or minim)

Q: What is this mark over the B♭ in line 5?
A: It is an accent mark

Q: What does the dot above a note mean?
A: Play the note short or *staccato*

Instrument question:
Q: How do you get distortion from most standard amps?
A: You turn down the volume and turn up the gain

Grade 4

The theory questions here refer to the performance piece 'Rage Against Everything', pages 10-11.

Q: What is the difference between the two markings at the beginning of bars three and four?
A: Bar three contains a sharp sign and bar four is a natural sign

Q: What do the markings '*f*' and '*mp*' mean?
A: Loud and moderately quiet (*forte* & *mezzo piano*)

Q: In bar 20, what type of notes are these and what does 'pm' mean?
A: These are sixteenth notes (semiquavers) and 'pm' means palm muting

Q: Explain what you do at the D.C. al Coda marking
A: At this point you return to the beginning and play until you see the Coda sign and then skip to the Coda

Instrument question:
Q: How would you tune your guitar without using a tuner?
A: Tune to the fifth/fourth fret or use harmonics

Grade 5

The theory questions here refer to the performance piece 'All Funked Up', pages 10-11.

Q: What do these signs mean in bar one, line three?
A: A slide and an accent

Q: Explain how you would construct a dominant seventh chord
A: A dominant 7th chord is made up of the root, major 3rd, perfect 5th and flattened 7th notes of a major scale

Q: Name the pitches of the two notes in bar one, line four
A: C♯ and E

Q: What is another name for a 5 chord (eg A5)?
A: A power chord

Instrument question:
Q: Which position would you choose on your pick up selector for this piece? What type of sound are you creating?
A: The neck pick up will give you the brighter tone found in funk rhythm

Grade 6

The theory questions here refer to the performance piece 'Big, Big, Big', pages 4-5.

Q: Can you point out and describe three physical/expressive techniques in this piece?
A: Palm muting, vibrato and bends

Q: The direction *to neck pickup* at bar 25 creates a more mellow sound. Why is this?
A: The aim is create variety in the overdrive sound at a point where the song shifts to a higher register

Q: How is a minor 9th chord constructed?
A: Root, minor 3rd, perfect 5th, minor 7th and 9th

Q: Could you please tell me the notes of an A harmonic minor scale?
A: A, B, C, D, E, F, G♯, A or tone equivalent

Instrumental question:
Q: What is a truss rod used for in a guitar?
A: The truss rod is a part of a guitar used to stabilise the profile (or 'relief') of the neck. Usually it is a steel rod running inside the neck and has a bolt used for adjustment of tension.

Grade 7

The theory questions here refer to the performance piece 'Third Degree', pages 10-13.

Q: Explain how the tapped harmonics technique works in bar 2
A: Tapped harmonics are an extension of the tapping technique. The note is fretted as usual, but instead of striking the string, the string is tapped at one of the places where natural harmonics occur.

Q: What are the notes of the G lydian mode?
A: G, A, B, C♯, D, E, F♯ and G

Q: In a Sus2 chord, what note is not often included?
A: The major third

Q: Name and demonstrate three techniques in this piece.
A: Bends, artificial harmonics and slides

Instrumental and history question:
Q: The piece is styled 'Van Halen Rock'. What can you tell me about this style?
A: Van Halen was a band formed by Edward van Halen and his brother Alex which had a great deal of success in the late 70s and throughout the 1980s. Edward van Halen is credited with revolutionising the sound of the guitar by his use of the tapping technique.

Grade 8

The theory questions here refer to the performance piece '667', pages 4-6.

Q: The Coda uses 4/4, 12/8 and 3/4. Can you please explain these to me?
A: The first is four quarter (crotchet) notes to the bar; the second is twelve eighth (quaver) notes to the bar and the third is three quarter notes to the bar

Q: What is the key signature in the 3/4 section?
A: Four sharps: F♯, C♯, G♯ and D♯

Q: This is in the key of E major. What note does the Aeolian mode begin on and how is it constructed?
A: C♯. The notes of the mode are: C♯, D♯, E, F♯, G♯, A, B and C♯

Q: What scale is being used in the sixteenth (semiquaver) note run in the last bar on line 3, page 4?
A: The E natural minor scale

Instrumental and history question:
Q: Tell me about heavy metal music and name some important performers in this style
A: Heavy metal grew out of heavy rock in the late 60s with bands such as Led Zeppelin and Deep Purple. It is characterised by use of heavily distorted guitars, driving rhythms and a dense bass and drum style. There are now many different sub-genres of the music and it remains one of the most popular music forms in rock. Modern performers would include Metallica and Marilyn Manson.

Guitar Notation Explained

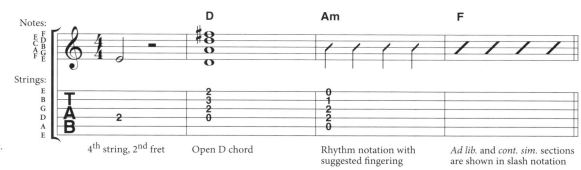

THE MUSICAL STAVE shows pitches and rhythms and is divided by lines into bars. Pitches are named after the first seven letters of the alphabet.

TABLATURE graphically represents the guitar fingerboard. Each horizontal line represents a string, and each number represents a fret.

Notes:

Strings:

4th string, 2nd fret | Open D chord | Rhythm notation with suggested fingering | *Ad lib.* and *cont. sim.* sections are shown in slash notation

Definitions For Special Guitar Notation

HAMMER ON: Pick the lower note, then sound the higher note by fretting it without picking.

PULL OFF: Pick the higher note then sound the lower note by lifting the finger without picking.

SLIDE: Pick the first note, then slide to the next with the same finger.

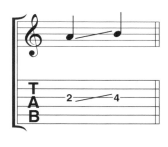

STRING BENDS: Pick the first note then bend (or release the bend) to the pitch indicated in brackets.

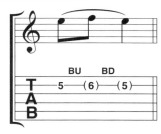

GLISSANDO: A small slide off of a note toward the end of its rhythmic duration. Do not slide 'into' the following note – subsequent notes should be repicked.

VIBRATO: Vibrate the note by bending and releasing the string smoothly and continuously.

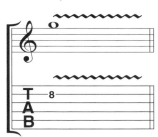

TRILL: Rapidly alternate between the two bracketed notes by hammering on and pulling off.

NATURAL HARMONICS: Lightly touch the string above the indicated fret then pick to sound a harmonic.

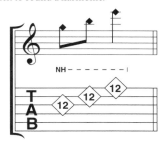

PINCHED HARMONICS: Bring the thumb of the picking hand into contact with the string immediately after the pick.

PICK HAND TAP: Strike the indicated note with a finger from the picking hand. Usually followed by a pull off.

FRET HAND TAP: As pick hand tap, but use fretting hand. Usually followed by a pull off or hammer on.

QUARTER TONE BEND: Pick the note indicated and bend the string up by a quarter tone.

PRE-BENDS: Before picking the note, bend the string from the fret indicated between the staves, to the equivalent pitch indicated in brackets in the TAB

WHAMMY BAR BEND: Use the whammy bar to bend notes to the pitches indicated in brackets in the TAB

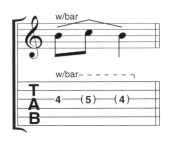

D.%. al Coda

D.C. al Fine

- Go back to the sign (%), then play until the bar marked *To Coda* ⊕ then skip to the section marked ⊕ *Coda*.

- Go back to the beginning of the song and play until the bar marked *Fine* (end).

- Repeat bars between signs.

- When a repeated section has different endings, play the first ending only the first time and the second ending only the second time.